# FUN & FUNKY
# Fingers
## and
## Toes

# MARIE MINGAY

D&S
BOOKS

First published in 2001 by D&S Books

© 2001 D&S Books

D&S Books
Cottage Meadow, Bocombe,
Parkham, Bideford
Devon, England
EX39 5PH

e-mail us at:-
enquiries.dspublishing@care4free.net

This edition printed 2001

ISBN 1-903327-30-X

Creative Director: Sarah King
Editor: Yvonne Worth
Project Editor: Anna Southgate
Designer: Axis Design
Photography: Paul Forrester

Distributed in the UK & Ireland by
Bookmart Limited
Desford Road
Enderby
Leicester LE9 5AD

Distributed in Australia by
Herron Books
39 Commercial Road
Fortitude Valley
Queensland 4006

1 3 5 7 9 10 8 6 4 2

# contents

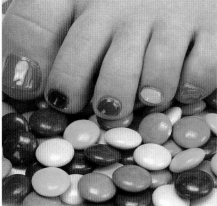

# Introduction

Emery boards come in all sorts of fun designs.

Once upon a time little girls' storybooks were full of fairy tales and magical creatures. This book is packed full of its own type of magic as it teaches you step-by-step nail art and fantastic designs just like mum wears. In today's world it is not only fashion-conscious teenagers and adults who wear polish and nail art – move over mum, we kids have our own stuff too!

As the nail industry has become increasingly popular, the range of products has grown enormously. There are now collections of designer nail art kits for children from 5 years old to teenagers. Basic manicure kits include a nail dryer, self-adhesive nails, nail polishes, cool transfers/decals, manicuring trays and emery boards. More advanced kits, aimed at 9 year olds to teenagers, contain a wide range of products from glitter polishes, nail jewellery, transfers/decals,

Glittering polishes can be pretty and are easy to apply.

This is how you do it!

6

Girls just want to have fun!

foil strips, brush paint, sticker sheets and lots more! You are limited only by your own imagination, so be adventurous. Using everything that shimmers and shines you can create your own fairy-tale designs.

   This book also offers some fun ways of keeping your nails healthy and strong, tips for nail-biters, a basic introduction to manicuring your nails and diet tips to keep your nails healthy and in good condition. These tips are very simple and you can have lots of fun creating your own recipes for healthy nails. Milkshakes taste really good! Get mum to help you liquidise cherries into your shake – it not only tastes delicious but is great for your nails too. Jelly is also excellent for your nails, so try to eat a cube a day straight from the packet (not quite as nice as jelly and ice cream but, nevertheless, you will see the results within a couple of months). Finally, remember to drink plenty of milk.

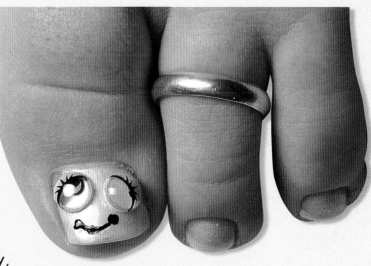

There are all kinds of fun stick-on accessories to add to your nails!

7

# Healthy nails

White spots are very common and can be caused by a lack of zinc in your diet or by nail damage. To avoid them, eat a healthy diet and avoid banging your nails!

One of the very first things people notice about others is the state and condition of their nails. It is, therefore, very important to learn all the methods involved in caring for your nails along with the techniques of nail decoration. Essentially, there are two main steps to follow in order to have healthy nails:
1. Nutrition (eating a healthy diet).
2. Caring for your nails (moisturising, manicures and avoiding knocking them).

# Nutrition

In order to grow healthy, strong nails you need to eat a healthy, well-balanced diet. Nails need protein, vitamins and minerals to grow properly. Warmer weather encourages nails to grow faster whereas lack of essential nutrients slows nail growth down.

## Vitamin A

This vitamin aids nail growth and can be found in green vegetables, carrots, tomatoes, apricots and cherries.

## Calcium

This is important for strength and helps develop strong bones and nails. It is found in foods such as fish and milk and in other dairy products such as yoghurt, cheese and butter.

## Iodine

Iodine is also needed for nail growth and is found in fish, spinach and watercress.

## Sulphur

Sulphur is essential for nail consistency. This is a mineral and is found in cabbage, onions and cucumbers.

# Caring for your nails

The main way to keep your nails healthy is to have a regular manicure – making sure your hands and nails are well moisturised as well. This is something that can be fun to do with friends – take it in turns to do each other's nails – and then experiment with the different projects in this book!

## Basic nail manicure

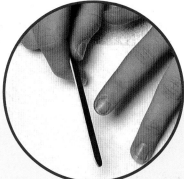

1

First make sure your nails are completely clean and dry.

2

File in one direction only, using a sweeping action. Never saw in a back-and-forth motion. Always work from the sides to the middle of your nail as shown.

3

Now you need a cotton bud. You can make your own by taking an orange stick and wrapping the tip in a few strands from a cotton pad.

**4** Apply a generous amount of cuticle remover, cream or oil. Massage using circular movements around the cuticles.

**5** Use your cotton bud to clean under your nails.

**6** Then use the cotton bud to push back your cuticles – be very gentle!

**7** Now you need some hand cream – squirt some into the palm of your hand.

**8** Now massage the cream into your hands until it is all rubbed in, and your hands are nice and soft. After applying hand cream you must remove any left-over cream or oil from your nails by gently wiping cotton wool or a cotton pad, dipped in warm soapy water, over each nail.

**9**

Now use a buffer (these come in different styles) to smooth down your nails.

## tip

When applying a polish, roll the bottle (never shake it) between your hands to avoid any blobbing. Starting from the cuticle, use only two or three strokes to give you a smooth finish for your polish. Most nail polishes require two to three coats for a true colour.

**10**

Now apply your base-coat. Allow to dry thoroughly.

**11**

Next apply a coloured polish. Here we're using a pale pink opalescent polish that gives a nice natural look.

**12**

Finally, once your polish is dry, finish off with a clear topcoat.

# Equipment and materials

Natural emery boards, orange sticks and a buffer.

Children's nail art and teenage nail art come in a range of kits and designs. Most nail art and polish designed for five to ten year olds will only stay on the nail until you apply soap and water. When using these kits you can use a topcoat to help seal your design. Transfers and decals include those that stick on, rub on or water-based styles. All of them appear in the designs in this book. The best results are achieved by applying a topcoat (preferably a quick-drying variety) to seal your design.

The reason I advise using a topcoat is that nail polish and nail art usually takes anything from 30 to 60 minutes to dry properly. Some kits include a nail dryer, but even with these, artwork will still take a good 30 minutes to dry.

Plastic nails should always be applied with the adhesive tapes that are supplied with kits. Never use nail glue or superglue on any child under the age of ten.

Emery boards are used to gently shape your nail – always file in one direction, using sweeping strokes up each side of the nail towards the top, as shown in the Basic nail manicure (p9). Never file your nails after bathing as this is when they are at their softest and weakest.

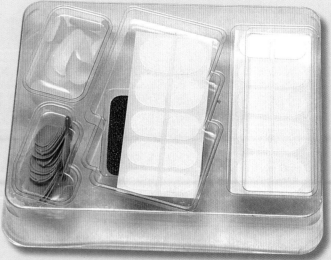

A typical kit you will find for false nails.

Nail art pens are an excellent way of creating your own designs.

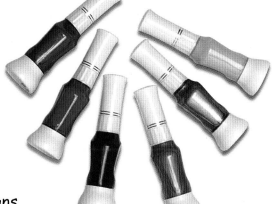

# Nail dryers

Nail dryers include aerosol cans, battery-operated nail dryers and quick-drying topcoats. Nails can take anything from 5 minutes to 30 minutes to become touch dry using a nail dryer.

# Nail stencils

Stencils are used by placing them over your painted nail, then using nail art pencils or brushes to create fun designs.

# Nail art pencils and paints

These can be used freehand or with a stencil as a guide. They are included in specialised kits and can create dazzling effects.

Polishes also come in fun shaped bottles!

Glitter polishes.

Brushes, paints and paint palette for nail art.

# Moisturisers

Moisturisers are essential to keep your nails strong and flexible so that they do not become dry, flaky or break easily.

# Nail accessory tools

To get started you will need your nail accessory tools! Here are some of the things you will need to take care of your nails along with instructions on how to use them.

## Nail files

There are different types of nail files; some have coarse surfaces and others have fine surfaces. Emery boards have a coarse surface and are used if you want to shorten your nails quickly, whilst sharpening them. Nail files with a fine surface are used to file a small amount of nail and to neaten rough edges.

## Nail scissors

Nail scissors have slightly curved short blades. Try not to use them too often as they can cause splitting. They are also very sharp – so take care. Nail scissors are used mainly to cut the length of a nail: the actual shaping is best done with a file.

Tweezers.

Emery boards.

## Buffers

Buffing encourages your nails to grow as it increases the flow of blood in the nail bed. It also takes off the dull top layers of the nail and builds up a shine. This leaves you with a smooth surface on which to apply nail polish.

There are a variety of buffers available, with a different surface coarseness on each side. Use the coarsest side sparingly. Try buffing your nails at least once every two weeks.

## Orange sticks

These sticks are used to gently push back your cuticles from the base of the nail. Always wrap the tip of your orange stick with cotton wool (as shown on p9). The cotton wool provides a much more gentle way of pushing back your cuticles.

Orange sticks are sometimes called cuticle sticks. As illustrated in Basic nail manicure (p9), after filing you can soak your nails in warm water or apply softening hand cream around your cuticles to avoid any damage.

Buffer

Scissors.

Orange sticks.

## Cuticle creams and oils

There are a wide variety of cuticle treatments available. They are used to soften the cuticle at the base of the nail (see the Basic nail manicure p9).

## Nail strengtheners

As the name suggests, strengtheners toughen your nails. You need to apply them first, before applying your basecoat. Always make sure you apply nail strengthener in the centre of your nail and not around the edge or to the cuticle as this can have a drying effect. Remember that you are trying to make your nails stronger, not dry out the surrounding skin or cuticle.

Gold and silver false nails.

Mini nail polish, lip gloss and body gems.

Basecoat and topcoats are essential whatever nail art you choose.

## Basecoat

Basecoat is used to give you a smooth surface on which to apply your polish, as well as to protect your nails and prevent brightly coloured polish from discolouring your nails.

## Topcoat

The topcoat acts as a protective layer over your nail polish and nail art. It also helps it last longer and gives it a super shine. Fast- or quick-drying topcoat is specially designed to dry much more quickly than the regular type.

## Nail potions

These are designed to help stop children biting their nails. They are only suitable for children over the age of three, and are very quick and easy to use. Simply dip your fingers into the magic sponge every day. This gives your nails a very bitter taste and will help you to stop biting your nails. These products also help to condition the skin around the nail and the cuticle, and encourage the nails to grow stronger.

# Polish effects

Using paints and polishes can be a quick and easy way to brighten up your nails. You can paint your nails all the same colour, or choose a different colour for each nail, using bright, even neon colours. There are also special polishes that change colour in different temperatures, as well as a really fun technique for creating a swirly marble-effect pattern. All these polishes are easy to remove, so there's nothing to stop you experimenting on yourself – and your friends!

# Feeling moody

YOU WILL NEED

Basecoat

Your designer polishes –
two or three
different colours

Quick-drying topcoat

Mood-change polishes are fantastic – when you are cold they go dark and when you are warm they are light again. You can have fun with two or more colours.

## tip

Try adding a decal for a different effect.

**2** Apply the first colour to your thumb. Here we're using a Lilac polish first.

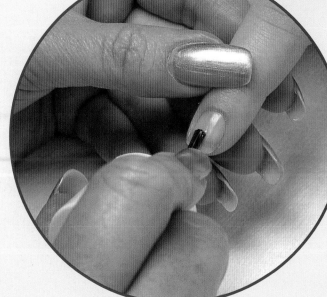

**1** First apply a basecoat and allow to dry.

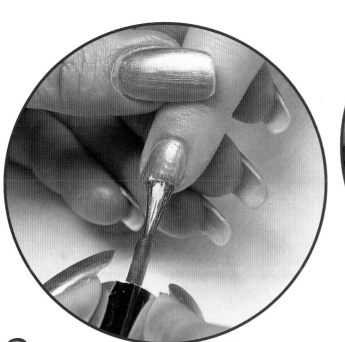

**3**

Next choose a second colour for a finger. Continue painting your other nails using different colours if you wish. It can take up to three coats to get a good colour.

**4**

Always remember to use a quick-drying topcoat.

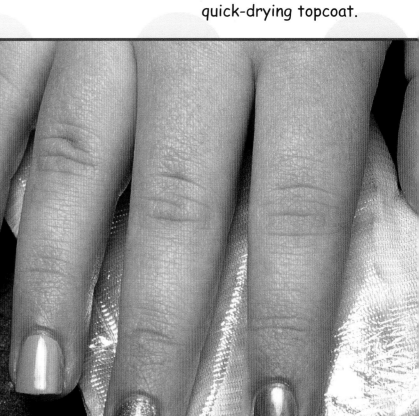

# Bright neon

Neons come in very bright colours, and some even glow in the dark. Great effects can be created using two or three different colours on your nails. Here we have chosen lemon and lime.

**2**

Apply lemon polish to alternate toenails.

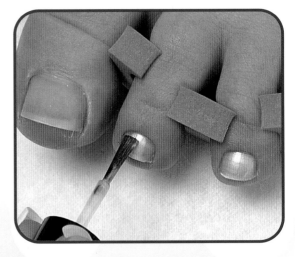

**3**

Next apply lime polish to the remaining nails.

**1**

Apply a basecoat and allow to dry completely.

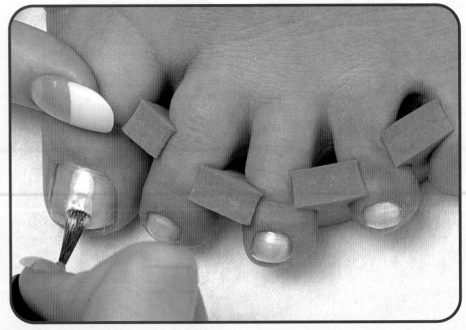

# 4

Choose your stickers – these brightly coloured glittery ones are ideal.

## tip

See pages 28 to 47 for more sticker and transfer ideas!

# 5

Position your sticker over the nail.

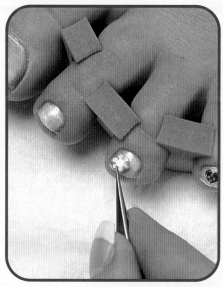

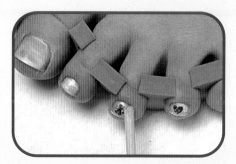

# 6

Pat the sticker firmly into place so that it stays on securely.

# 7

Apply a quick-drying topcoat.

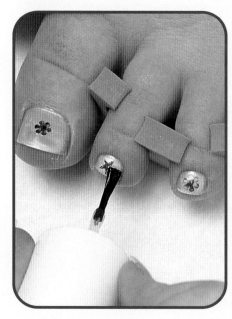

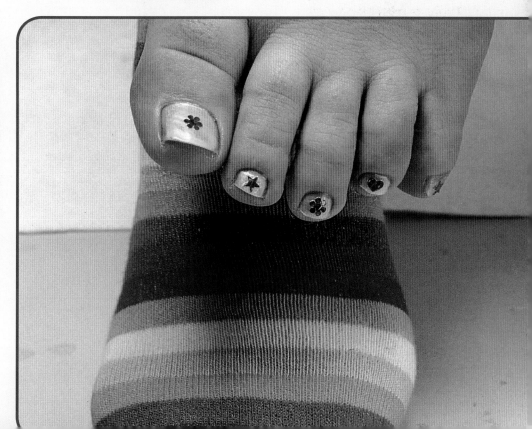

# Colour swirl

For this effect you will need a special marbling kit. Once you get the hang of it you can make patterns with any number of colours.

The marbling kit.

**1**

The marbling paints can stain your skin, and take ages to remove, so you need to rub a protective masking gel to the skin around your nail.

**2**

Apply some of the gel under your nail too, as it can stain and spoil the pattern.

## tip

Fill your cup with water that is at room temperature. If you use water that is too hot it will dry out your colours too quickly, whereas cold water will prevent the colours from developing properly.

# 3

Shake all your colours well. Place the first drop in the centre of the cup and allow the colour to spread out. Notice that the colour will spread. If it does not spread properly you will need to add a drop of marbling thinner into the colour bottle and shake well.

# 4

Repeat the process with the second and third colours.

# 5

Before the colours start to dry on the water's surface, quickly use a T-shaped pin to move your design around. You have around 20 to 60 seconds to create your design, although this time may vary depending on the temperature of the room.

23

# 6

Slowly dip a finger down through the design you have created on the water. You are now transferring exactly what you see on the surface of the water to your fingertip. Stop when your nail tip is fully covered with the design.

# 7

Remove your finger from the glass slowly and carefully, so the design will transfer smoothly to your nail.

# 8

Now, using the back of the T-shaped pin (flat part) or a cotton bud, skim off the excess colours around the water surface and wipe them onto a paper towel. Cover the cup with a lid when you have finished with the design. You can always use the same water for the next design.

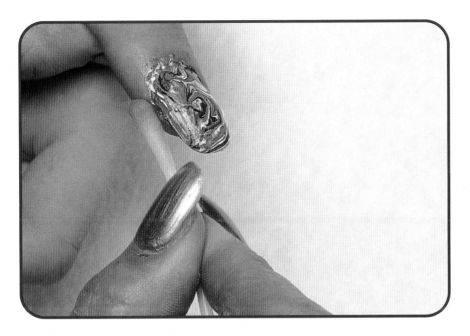

# 9

Allow the nail to dry and then use a paper towel to wipe off any excess colour from the finger itself. Using the marbling seal, lightly cover the entire nail design and allow it to dry.

## tip

This picture clearly shows how the swirly pattern sticks to your nail.

And here you can see how the colours stay on your nail as you remove it from the water.

# Sweet Feet

Here is a quick way to brighten up your nails – ideal for showing off your toes or fingers.

**1**

Apply basecoat to each nail, and allow it to dry completely.

**2**

Using your five different polishes paint each nail a different colour. Give each toenail two to three coats.

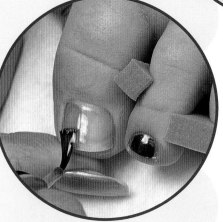

## tip

It can be difficult to paint your toenails without smudging them, so do use toe separators to hold the toes apart. They may feel a bit funny, but they're really useful!

**3**

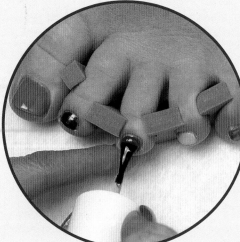

Once your polish is dry, apply a clear topcoat.

26

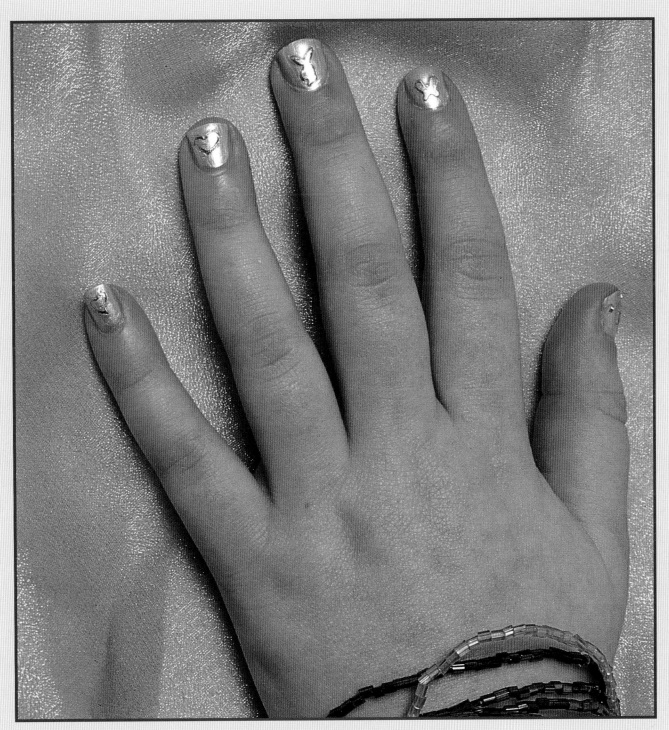

Here you can see how a simple polish effect can be made to
look even more special by adding a stick-on transfer or decal.

27

# Nail transfers and stickers

Decals come in a wide range of designs, including patterns for flowers, animals, scenes, zodiac signs and lots more. Some are available as water transfers and some as stick-on transfers or decals. With a little imagination, you can create different pictures by cutting up your transfers or decals and adding two or three to each nail as illustrated here. You could also add stick-on nail art, such as rhinestones and gems, for an extra glamorous effect.

# Musical toes

YOU WILL NEED

Toe Separators

Basecoat

Silver polish

Transfers

Tweezers

Quick-drying topcoat

Pale polishes provide an excellent base for summery designs. Show off your musical nails in sandals or bare feet – a different note for each toe!

1 Apply your basecoat and allow to dry thoroughly.

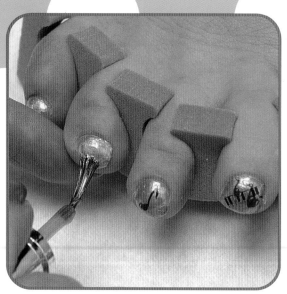

2 Apply two coats of silver polish, making sure each coat dries thoroughly.

3 Lift the transfer from its backing paper with tweezers.

## tip

These transfers are quite delicate – cut them out carefully – you don't want to spoil any!

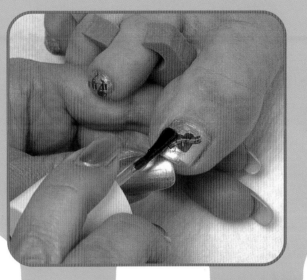

## 4

Place the transfer onto your nail, and then smooth it out using tweezers or an orange stick.

## 5

Apply a quick-drying topcoat to secure your design.

31

# Summer holidays

This is an ideal design for hot sunny days on the beach or on your summer holiday. And when the holiday's over, this design will bring back instant memories!

**1** First apply the basecoat and allow to dry thoroughly.

**2** Paint on two coats of the pail blue polish. Remember to let the polish dry between coats.

**3** Carefully cut out the transfer and soak it in water until it begins to slide from the backing paper.

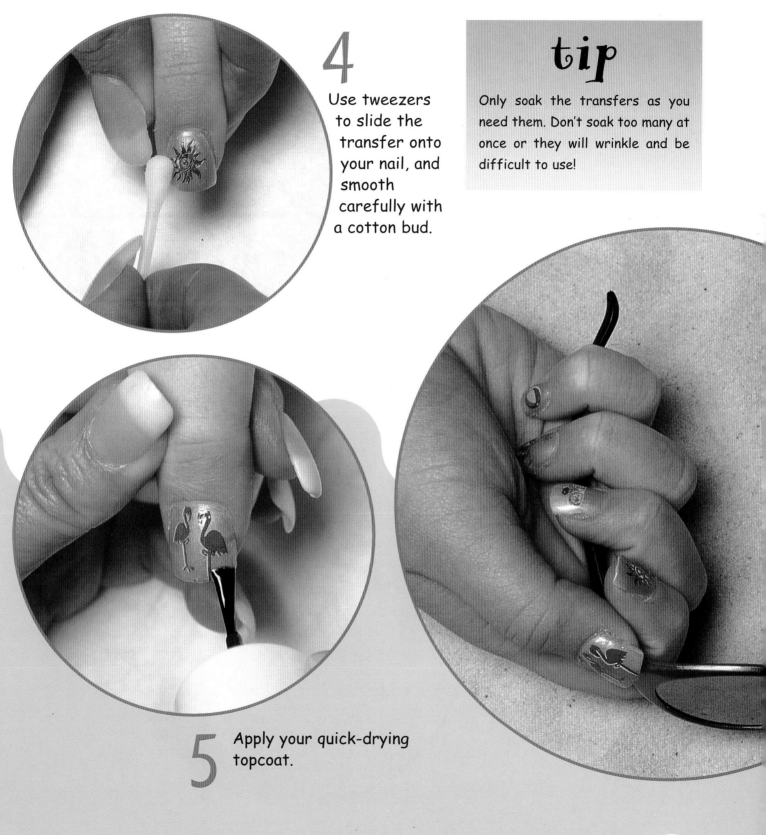

4 Use tweezers to slide the transfer onto your nail, and smooth carefully with a cotton bud.

**tip**

Only soak the transfers as you need them. Don't soak too many at once or they will wrinkle and be difficult to use!

5 Apply your quick-drying topcoat.

# Turning Japanese

## YOU WILL NEED

Basecoat

White nail polish

Cotton bud

Transfers/water decals

Scissors

Shallow bowl of water

Quick-drying topcoat

There are many decals with images from different countries. You can pick them to match a place you've been on holiday, or a particular outfit. Here we've chosen an oriental look.

1

Apply basecoat and, once it has dried, apply two coats of white nail polish.

2

If you smudge any polish onto your fingers, remove using a cotton bud dipped in polish remover.

**tip**

The more delicate these transfers are the more you will need to take your time in preparing them – do not rush!

3 Carefully cut out your transfer, soak it in the water and gently begin to slide it off the backing paper.

4 Slide the transfer onto your nail, moving it carefully into position.

5 You may need to trim the decal to fit your own nail size.

35

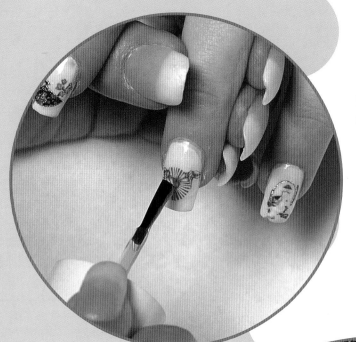

# 6

Once you have created your design, seal with quick-drying topcoat.

# Animal magic

YOU WILL NEED

Basecoat

Nail polish
(bright cerise pink)

Animal transfer

Scissors

Small shallow dish
of water

Cotton bud

Quick-drying topcoat

There are many transfers and stickers available with all sorts of animals. Simply choose your animal, pick a bright polish and you could have a zoo on your hands!

1

Apply basecoat and allow to dry.

2

Apply two coats of nail polish. Allow to dry for approximately five minutes.

3

Cut out your transfer, and soak it in water until it begins to slide off.

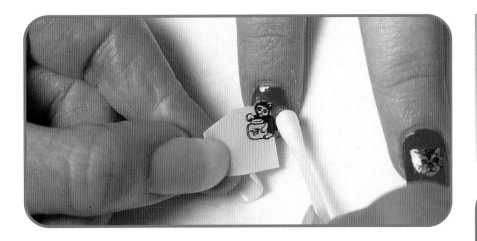

# tip

To make sure that you don't smudge your polish, always keep your cotton bud quite moist.

4 Position the transfer over your nail, and slide gently into place.

5 Use a cotton bud to smooth out any wrinkles in the transfer, and to move back into place if necessary.

6 Apply quick-drying topcoat as shown. Always try to apply your topcoat very lightly to avoid smudging your design.

# Cheeky monkey

### YOU WILL NEED

Basecoat

Nail polish (bronze)

Art tape

Scissors

Tweezers

Monkey sticker

Cotton bud

Quick-drying topcoat

This is another cute design that combines stickers with art tape. The art tape is quite easy to use – you just need to make sure you secure the ends firmly so they don't catch on your clothes.

**1** Apply basecoat and two coats of your chosen nail polish. Allow to dry for approximately five minutes.

**2** Once the polish is dry, stick a strip of art tape across your nail. Trim the ends to fit your nail.

**3** Use tweezers to remove the sticker from its backing paper.

**4**

Place the sticker onto your nail. You want to make it look as if the monkey is hanging from a branch!

**tip**

The art tape can be a bit tricky to put on your nail. It may be easier if you can get a friend to help you.

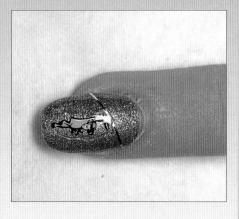

**5**

Use a cotton bud to pat your sticker into place and to remove any wrinkles.

**6** Finally apply a quick-drying topcoat to hold your monkey in place!

# Kiss and tell

A cute and girly design which combines different sizes of stickers, so you need to make sure you check the size you need before trying to apply them.

**1** Apply basecoat and allow to dry thoroughly.

**2** Apply two coats of pale pink polish, allowing each coat to dry thoroughly.

**3** Cut out your stick-on transfers and use tweezers to remove the first sticker from the backing paper.

**tip**
To check the size of the stickers you need for each nail, simply cut out around the sticker and lay it on the nail to make sure it will fit.

**4** Place the sticker on your nail.

**5** Secure in place with the orange stick.

**7**

Always remember to use quick-drying topcoat.

**6**

Now add the stars, using the same technique.

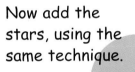

# Ducking around

## YOU WILL NEED

Basecoat

Colour polish

Stick-on transfers/decals

Tweezers

Cotton bud

Art pens/pencils

Quick-drying topcoat

This is a cute design that also lets you try some freehand painting. If you're not too confident, you can just leave the transfers on their own, or read the next chapter for some painting advice!

1
Apply basecoat and allow to dry thoroughly.

2
Paint on two coats of your chosen colour polish and leave to dry.

44

3

Using tweezers, gently peel off the duck sticker.

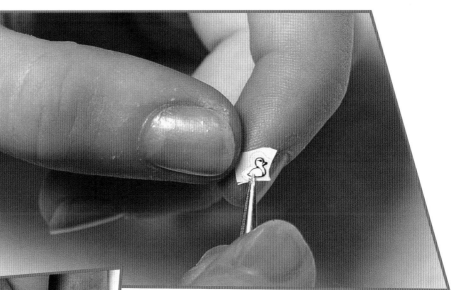

4

Stick your duck onto the nail, positioning it carefully.

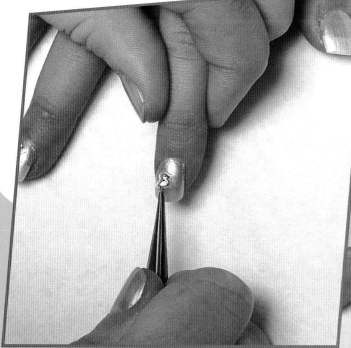

5

Smooth out any wrinkles in the sticker.

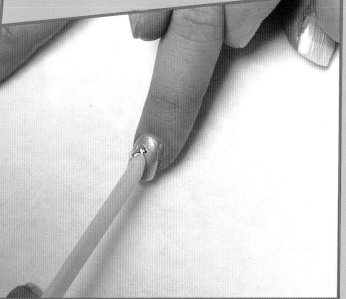

45

## tip

This freehand design is very simple – if you make a mistake, simply wipe away the nail paint before it dries, and start again.

**6** For the finishing touch, you can create your own duck pond using an art pen/paint.

**7** Always remember to use your quick-drying topcoat so that your ducks don't swim away!

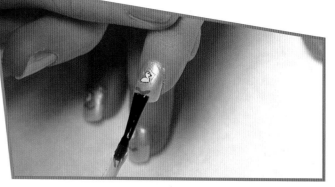

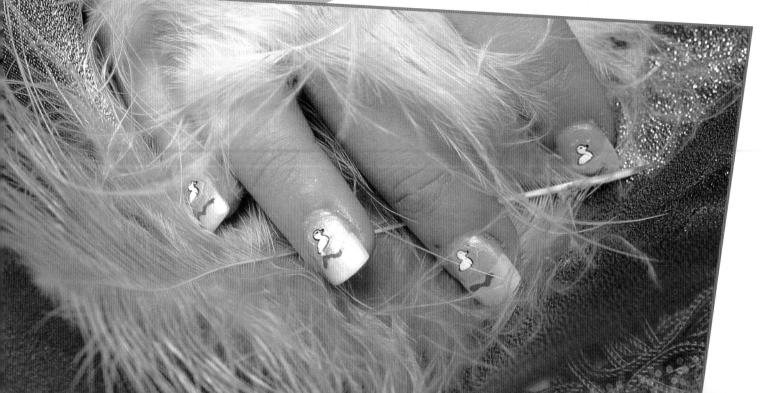

Nail transfers can be found to illustrate
every country in the world.

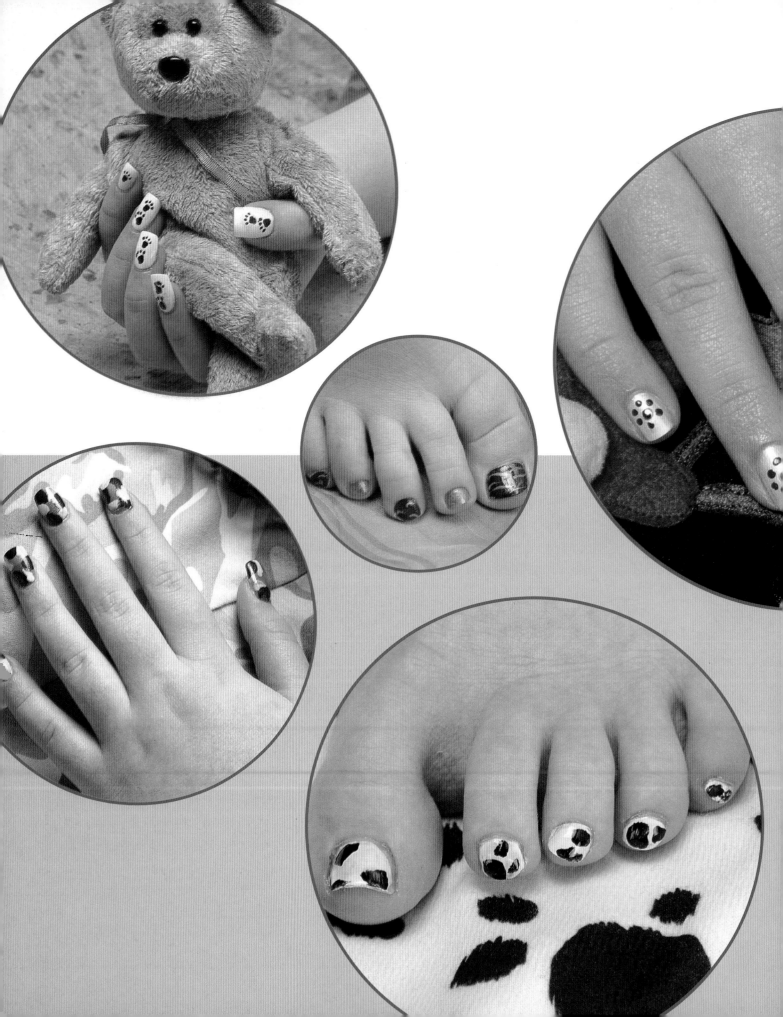

# Painting designs

You may want to create different pictures and patterns on your nails with paints instead of using stickers or transfers. There are several different ways of doing this. You can use nail art pens or brushes to paint freehand designs onto your nails. Some designs, such as simple spots or stripes are quite easy, while for others you need a steady hand to make sure your paint is evenly applied. If you're not confident about your painting ability, why not try a stencil, as shown in the first project?

# Stencils

YOU WILL NEED

Basecoat

Nail polish – white and another colour

Stencil pack

Tweezers

Quick-drying topcoat

Stencils come in a variety of designs, including hearts, flowers and more fun designs like the paw prints shown here. It can be great fun to create different looks and designs of your own.

1 Apply basecoat and allow to dry thoroughly.

2 Now paint at least two coats of white polish over each nail.

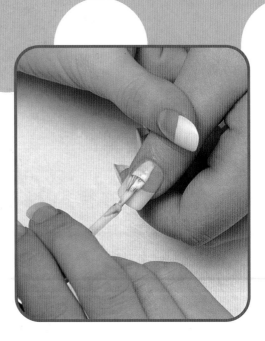

3 Choose a stencil design that is the right size for the nail, and peel the stencil from its backing.

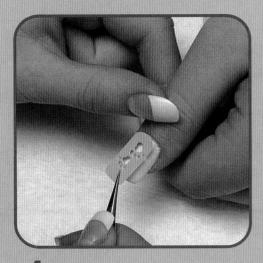

tip

Don't be too impatient to remove the stencil – if it smudges you will have to start all over again!

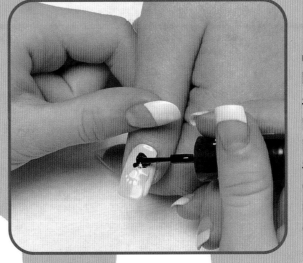

**4**

Place your stencil in the centre of your fingernail, and gently press it into place to make sure it does not move.

**5**

Now using your second colour polish, carefully paint over the stencil. Allow to dry for about a minute so that it does not smudge.

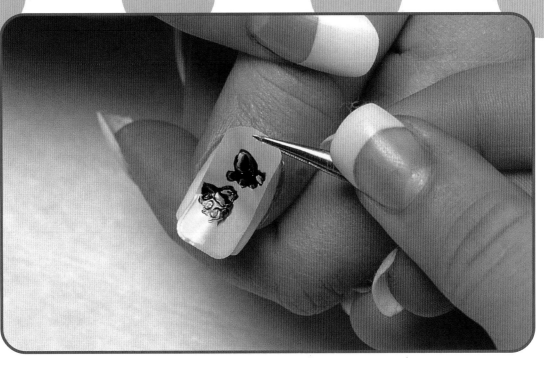

**6**

Carefully peel back the stencil to reveal your design.

7

As always, apply a final layer
of quick-drying topcoat.

# Camouflage

**YOU WILL NEED**

Basecoat

Nail polish (3 colours)

Quick-drying topcoat

Camouflage design is a very fashionable style, using colours ranging from traditional green, brown and black to bright red, green and gold. You can easily create this design on your nails as shown.

## tip

The camouflage pattern should smudge lightly at the edges, but make sure you wait until the colour polishes are completely dry before applying topcoat.

**1** Apply basecoat and your first choice of colour. Then paint on some spots of a different colour.

**2** Then add some splodges of a third colour, lightly smudging in your pattern as shown, building up your design in stages.

**3** Always seal with quick-drying topcoat. For a little extra glitz for that special jungle party, you can always add some holographic glitter!

# Dalmatian spots

**YOU WILL NEED**

Toe separators

Basecoat

White and black nail polishes

Quick-drying topcoat

Use two or three different polishes to create animal prints. Here we've used black and white polishes for a Dalmatian dog effect.

**1** First apply a basecoat to each toenail.

**2** When this has dried, apply two or three coats of white polish. Allow this to dry thoroughly.

**3** Using your black polish, as shown, place dabs of nail polish to create the spotty pattern.

## tip

If you do not have toe separators, you can use a tissue to keep your nails apart – as we have done here.

**4** When your polish is completely dry, remember your topcoat.

54

# Chocolate orange

**YOU WILL NEED**

Toe separators

Basecoat

Brown and orange polishes

Quick-drying topcoat

Here is another design we've done on toes, but this will work just as well on fingers – or why not try both! For added effect, try freehand painting some spots or stripes in contrasting colours.

## tip

You may find it is difficult to paint the designs on every nail as toenails can be very small! So why not just paint the designs on your big toes?

1

First apply a basecoat to each toenail, and allow to dry.

2

Then apply the orange polish to alternate nails.

3

Then apply the brown polish to the remaining nails.

**4** Paint some brown stripes onto the orange nails.

**5** Then paint some orange spots onto the brown nails.

**6** Finally seal with a clear topcoat.

# Jewelled flower

This design uses both nail paints and nail gems to create a pretty flower design. It's quite easy, but you do need to keep your hand steady! Bright colours will look most effective, as we've used here.

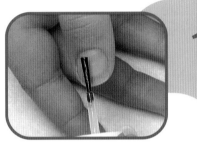

1 Apply basecoat and allow to dry thoroughly.

2

Apply two coats of bright yellow polish to each nail. Leave the second coat slightly tacky.

3

Use the orange stick to carefully pick up one of the gems.

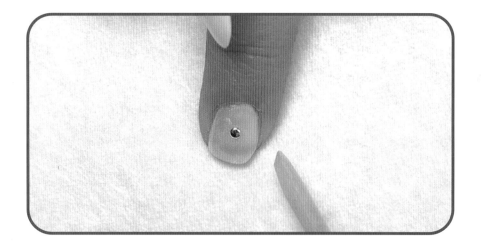

## tip

Although usually you want your polish to dry completely before applying nail art, for this project you need to keep the last colour coat a bit sticky so that the gem will stick to it.

4 Place the gem in the centre of your fingernail, as shown.

5 Take your art pen and draw in petals as shown.

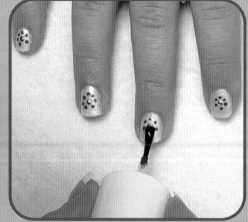

6 Always remember to use quick-drying topcoat.

# Noughts and crosses

YOU WILL NEED

Basecoat

White nail polish

Black nail art pen
or brush

Quick-drying topcoat

This is a fun design based on a popular game. If you're feeling really confident, why not try and fill in the grid at the end? Think of other games you could use as inspiration – snakes and ladders for example.

## tip

If you find the art pens difficult to use, you may find it easier to use an art brush.

1
Apply basecoat and allow to dry.

2
Apply two coats of white nail polish. Allow to dry for approximately five minutes.

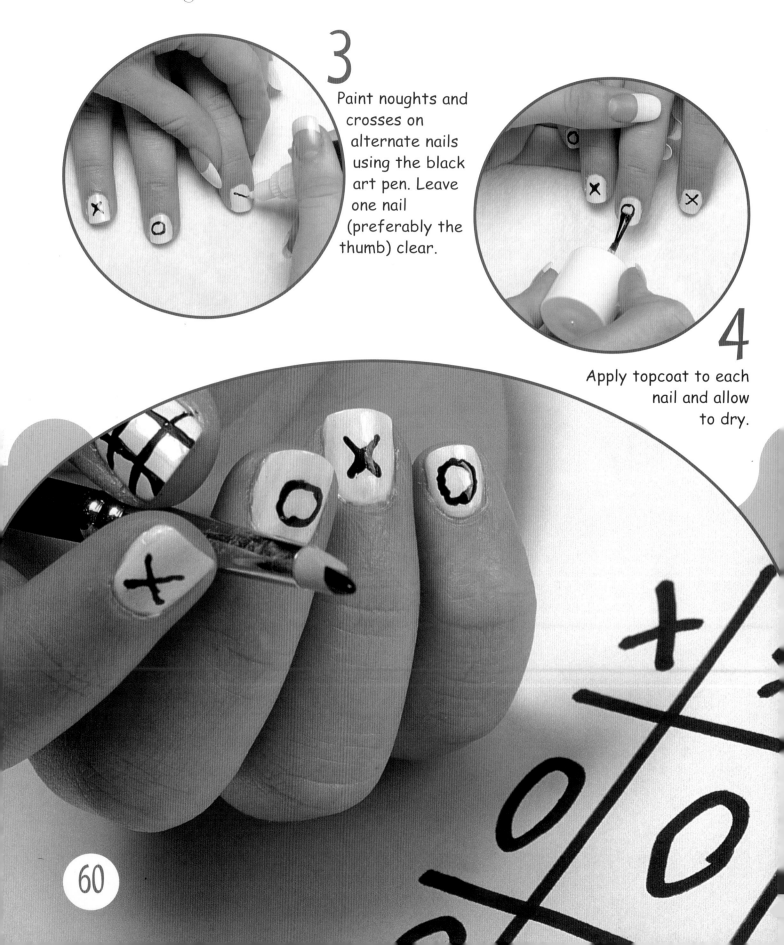

**3**

Paint noughts and crosses on alternate nails using the black art pen. Leave one nail (preferably the thumb) clear.

**4**

Apply topcoat to each nail and allow to dry.

You can paint all sorts of designs on your
nails. This is a lovely design for summer!

61

# Glitter effects

For parties and other special occasions, sparkling finger and toenails can add the perfect finishing touch to your outfit. There are different ways you can add glitter effects to your nails. The easiest is simply to use a glitter polish – these come in different colours and textures. Some glitter polishes are quite thick and take much longer to dry. There are also special polishes that glow and shimmer under bright lights. For added sparkle you can use rhinestones and other gems.

# Shimmering pearls

### YOU WILL NEED

Toe Separators

Basecoat

Shimmering pearl nail polish (1 or 2 colours)

Holographic polish

Quick-drying topcoat

Shimmering pearls are a range of designer polishes that contain two-tone glitter and can be great fun. Use one or two different colours, as illustrated, on your fingernails or toenails.

## *tip*

Here we've used a holographic polish which looks amazing under bright lights!

**1** Apply basecoat and allow to dry thoroughly.

**2** Choose one or two colours of polish, and apply to each nail.

**3** Don't forget your quick-drying topcoat.

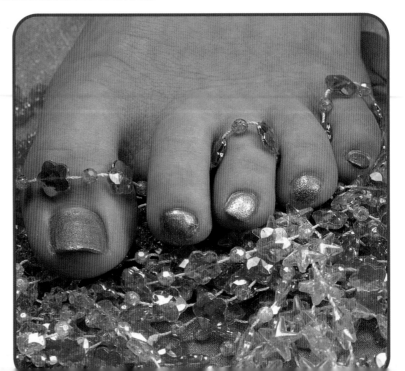

# Sparkle and shine

**YOU WILL NEED**

Toe separators

Basecoat

Red polish

Glitter polish

Quick-drying topcoat

This design is fun and bright and ideal for both toes and fingers. It is a very simple way to add some colour and sparkle, and will certainly get you noticed!

**1** Apply basecoat and allow to dry thoroughly.

**2** Next apply two coats of your chosen colour. Here we have used red but the choice is up to you.

**3** Paint the glitter polish at an angle across the nail, from one side of the nail to the other.

65

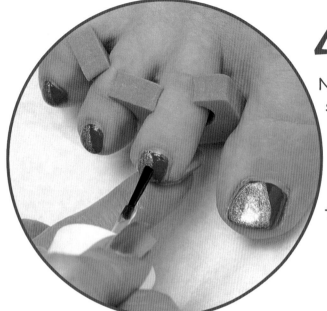

**4**

Never let the shimmer twinkle away, always seal with quick-drying topcoat.

## tip

Paint the glitter polish at the opposite angle on the other hand and foot to give a contrasting effect. Then team with sparkly accessories!

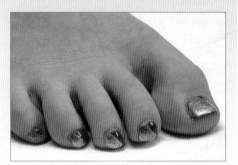

66

# Lilac gold

YOU WILL NEED

Toe separators

Basecoat

Coloured polish

Gold glitter polish

Orange stick

This is a sophisticated shimmering design that is ideal for parties and special occasions. Use a glitter polish as a topcoat for an extra sparkle.

1

Apply basecoat and allow to dry thoroughly.

2

Next apply two coats of lilac polish. Allow to dry thoroughly for about five minutes.

3

Now use two further polish colours. These should be metallic polishes, for a shimmering effect.

## tip

If you smudge or smear polish on your fingers or toes use an orange stick to remove it.

**4**

Apply quick-drying topcoat – here we've used a glitter polish for added effect.

# Black and white

**YOU WILL NEED**

Basecoat

Black and white nail polish

Rhinestones

Orange stick

Quick-drying topcoat

A French manicure is an elegant style, but you can create a dramatic alternative using black and white polishes. This project includes rhinestones to add extra sparkle.

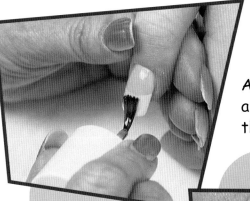

## 1

Apply a layer of basecoat and allow to dry thoroughly.

## *tip*

Using an orange stick is the easiest way to pick up and place each stone. Dampen the end of the stick, and pick up each rhinestone in turn.

## 3

Using the black polish you can make a black tip just like the reverse of a white and pink French polish. Take your time as you do this to make sure the line is nice and straight.

## 2

Now cover the whole of each nail with white polish. Again, allow to dry thoroughly.

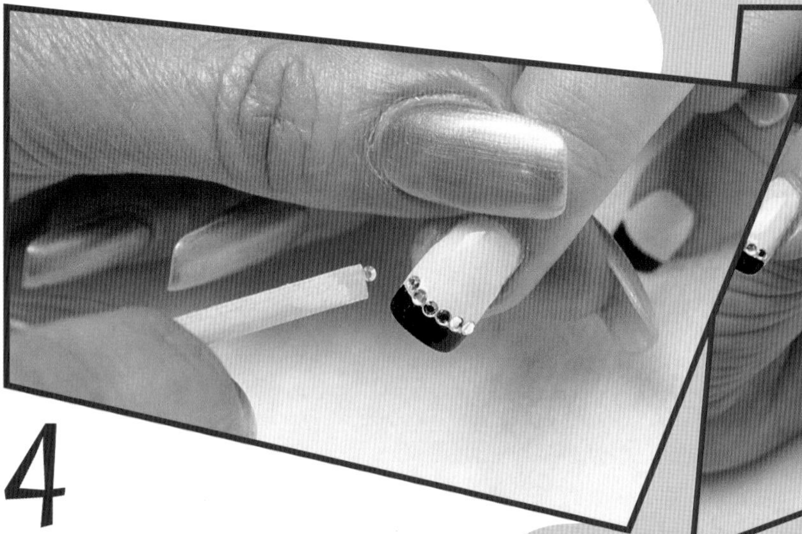

**4**

If you want to add some sparkle, you can use rhinestones to one or more of your nails. Apply each rhinestone carefully, while the black polish is still sticky.

**5**

Always remember to use a topcoat to finish.

Glitter polish goes well with strong dark
colours, and is ideal for both fingers and toes.

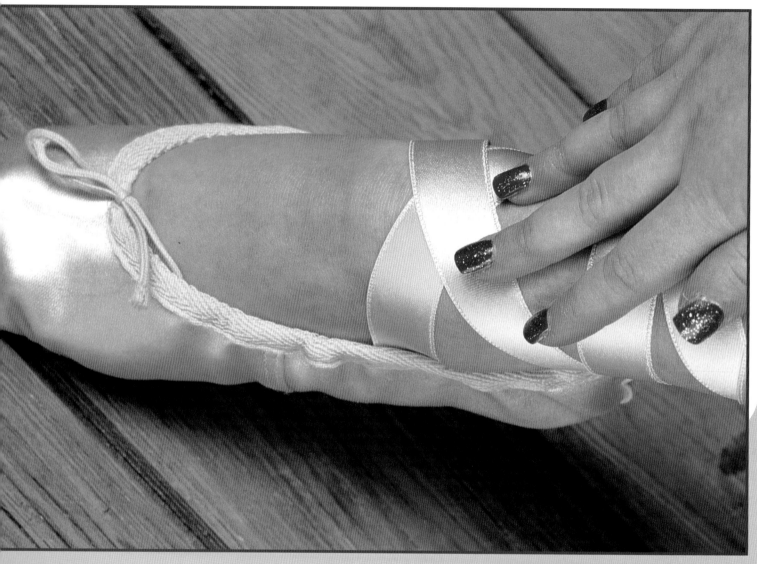

Glitter polishes are brilliant for special occasions.

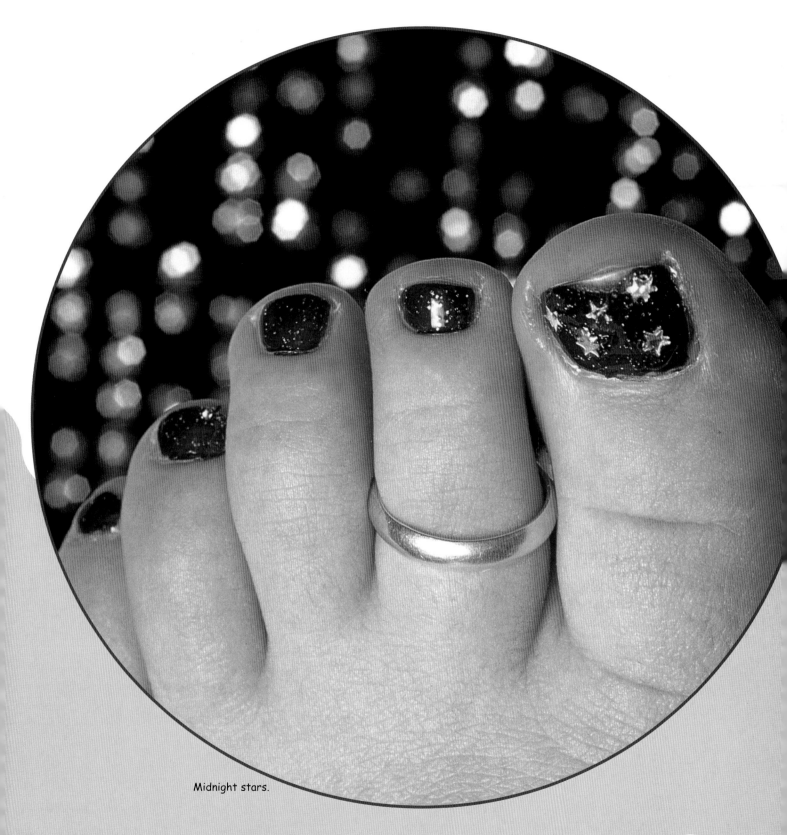

Midnight stars.

# Stick-on art projects

Stick-on nail designs, jewels and accessories come in a wide range of subjects, including stars, eyes and art tapes, and can be fun to use to create many different ideas. You can add glittering polishes too, and even more rhinestones!

# Star quality

**YOU WILL NEED**

Basecoat

Red polish

Foil tape

Scissors

Orange stick

Stars

Tweezers

Quick-drying topcoat

For added effect, why not match your stick-on design with some body jewellery? Both are simple to apply – and just as easy to remove!

**3**
Carefully cut out your art tape and place it across your nail as shown. It will stick well to the tacky surface.

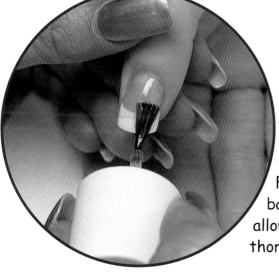

**2** Then add two coats of red polish. Allow the first to dry fully, but leave the second coat slightly tacky.

**1** First apply a basecoat and allow to dry thoroughly.

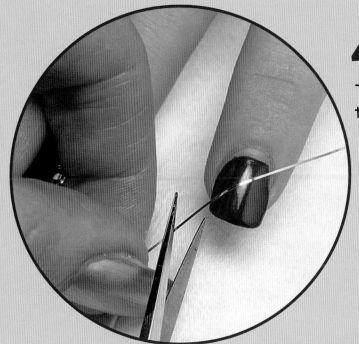

**4**
Trim both ends of the art tape to fit the nail.

**5**
Then secure the ends closely with the orange stick, so that they will not catch on your clothes.

# tip

When trimming the tape at the edge of your fingernail, always be careful not to cut yourself. You may be better off getting a parent or friend to do this for you.

**6**
Lift the stars from their backing paper, making sure they do not tear.

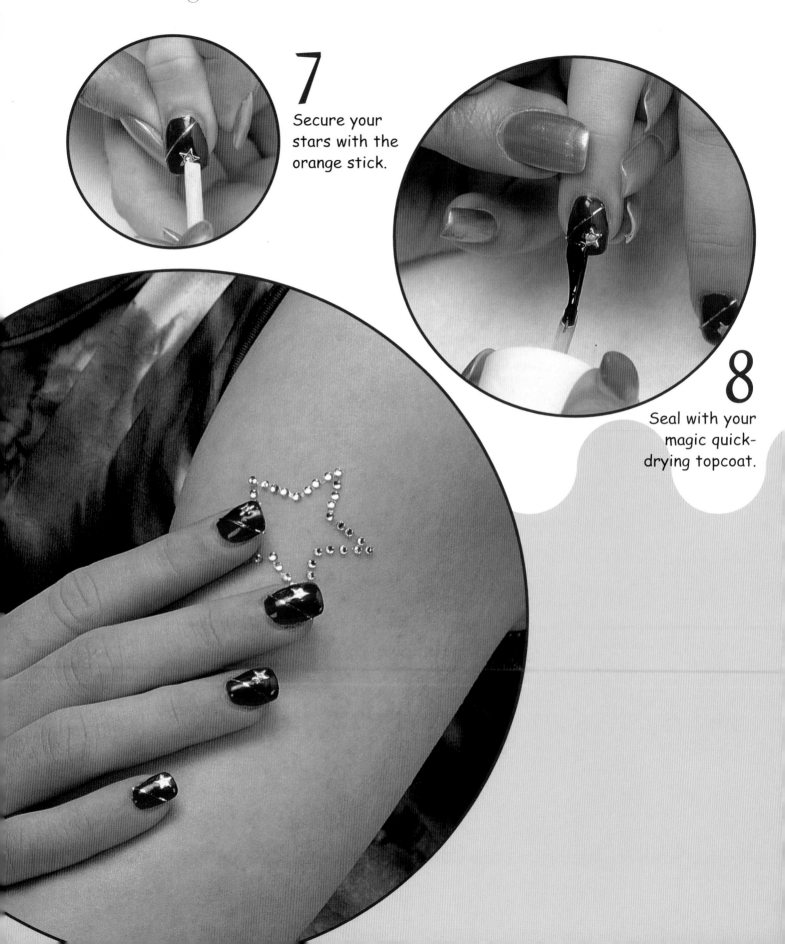

## 7
Secure your stars with the orange stick.

## 8
Seal with your magic quick-drying topcoat.

# Fairy dust

### YOU WILL NEED

French manicure polish

Glitter polish

Silver art tape

Scissors

Rhinestones

Small container

Orange stick

Cotton bud

Quick-drying topcoat

This project uses rhinestones and glitter polish for a sparkling effect. You will need a steady hand to apply the rhinestones as they are very small and fiddly.

## 1

First apply French manicure polish to each nail tip. Allow to dry.

## 2

Paint your glitter polish over the whole nail. Don't let this dry completely – you need it slightly sticky.

## tip

Spread out your rhinestones in a shallow dish or container so that they are easier to pick up.

While the polish is still tacky, cut a length of art tape and place it across your nail as shown.

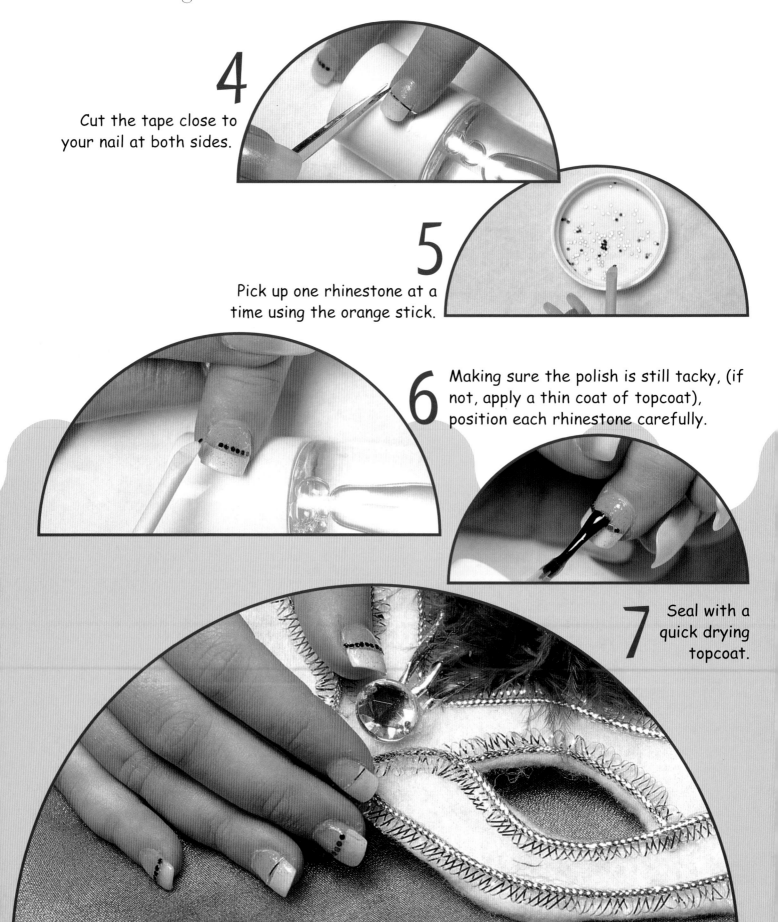

4 Cut the tape close to your nail at both sides.

5 Pick up one rhinestone at a time using the orange stick.

6 Making sure the polish is still tacky, (if not, apply a thin coat of topcoat), position each rhinestone carefully.

7 Seal with a quick drying topcoat.

# Magic stars

YOU WILL NEED

Basecoat

Lilac polish

Stars

Tweezers

Gems

Orange stick

Quick-drying topcoat

This project combines stick-on nail jewellery and gems for a magical effect. You need to take care, and be patient, as all the different bits will take time to put in place.

**1** First apply a basecoat, and allow to dry thoroughly.

**2** Then add two coats of lilac polish, allowing each coat to dry thoroughly.

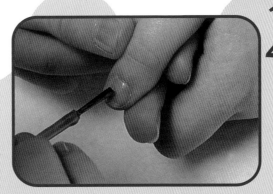

## tip

If your topcoat dries too quickly, simply dab a little into the centre of the star so the gem will stick.

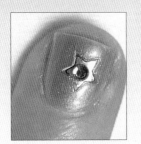

**3** Use the tweezers to remove the star jewels from their backing paper.

81

**4** Carefully place the star into the centre of your nail.

**5** Use the orange stick to smooth the star into place.

**6** Now apply a clear topcoat. Don't let this dry completely – you want it to be slightly sticky.

**7** Use the orange stick to pick up one of the gems.

**8** Place the gem into the centre of the star and finish with a second topcoat.

# False nail preparation

Not all nail kits come with good instructions. Follow these steps and, you will find they stay on better, and remove easily.

## tip

These nails make a perfect base for applying different types of nail art. If you want to leave the polished nails as they are, don't forget to apply a topcoat!

**1** You may need to trim the false nails.

**2** Use a small nail file to create a rough, grainy surface on your nail. Wipe away the nail dust.

**3** Stick the self-adhesive tapes provided with the kit to your natural nails - one at a time.

**4** Press the false nail onto this sticky tape, holding firmly to secure.

**5** When all nails are fitted securely, apply a coloured polish.

83

# Jungle feet

### YOU WILL NEED

Toe separators

A false nail set
(stick on)

Emery board

White block/buffer

You can buy all sorts of stick-on nails, and these ones are great fun. They feel slightly furry, and you can get them in different animal print designs.

**1** Check the size of each nail, and cut the stick-on to fit.

## tip

Always shape and file your toenails and buff them as you would if you were adding false nail extensions.

**2** Peel back the design from the backing, doing one at a time.

**3** Stick the tacky reverse side down onto your toenail and shape and push the stickers into place as shown.

# Handy hearts

These are more traditional false nails, and there are many different designs to choose from. You should always follow the instructions when applying, and also when you remove them (see p91)

## 1

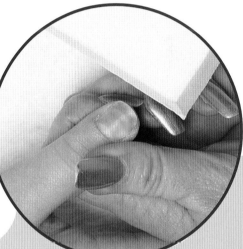

Shape, file and buff your nails before applying the false nails.

## tip

Clean off any glue from around your fingers or the nail using a damp cotton bud or tissue.

## 2

Brush off any nail dust so that the surface of your nail is clear and clean.

**3**

Paint the inside
of the first nail
with nail glue.

**4**

Stick the nail on, pushing
down firmly until it is securely
fixed. Repeat on other nails.

Just some of the fun stick-on accessories you can buy!

False nails come in all sorts of designs. Some are very glamorous!

Stick-on jewels can add a special
touch to ordinary polishes.

89

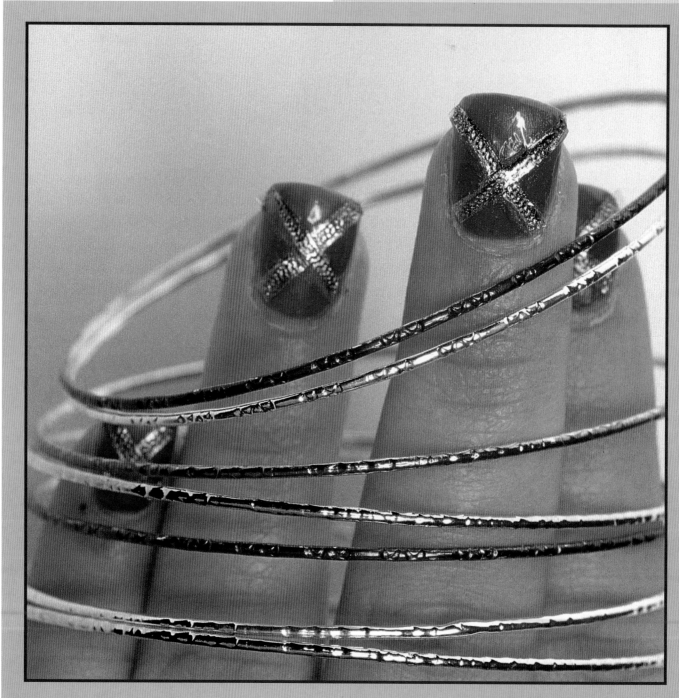

Art tapes can be used to make patterns on their own.

# Removing nail art

When removing plastic tips the same procedure applies as if you were removing your own nail art or plastic extensions applied with nail glue or self-adhesive nail art pads.

When using nail polishes that have to be removed with an actual nail polish remover, always choose a non-acetone polish remover. This will remove most types of nail art and polish together. You can also buy nail polish removing pads, which contain a conditioning Panthenol Pro-Vitamin B5.

The polishes that are featured in this book are professional products, but there are kits available commercially from chemists and toy stores, These polishes and nail art can be removed simply by using warm soapy water. For best results always use nail polishing removal pads with added Pro-Vitamin B5.

## Art tapes

These need to be removed with nail polish remover.

## Rhinestones and gems

These can be removed with nail polish remover, and you may need to use tweezers.

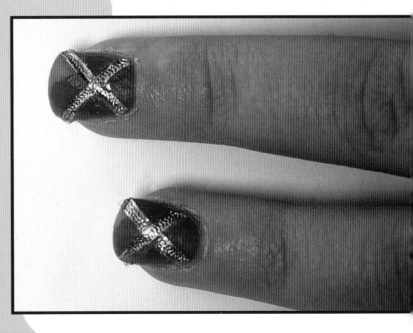

Neon crosses.

YOU WILL NEED

Acetone
(Nail polish remover)

Cotton pad

# Plastic tips

These can be removed with warm soapy water, gently increasing pressure around the free edges of the nails. There are also a number of kits available for the removal of false nails (plastic nail tips). The simplest and most effective way, however, is as follows.

## caution

Keep plastic nail tips away from extreme heat or naked flames. It is essential that the nails are never left glued onto your own nails for more than 24 hours, as this can cause damage to your natural nail. Never apply plastic nails to sore or infected nails or cuticles.

**1** 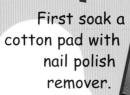 First soak a cotton pad with nail polish remover.

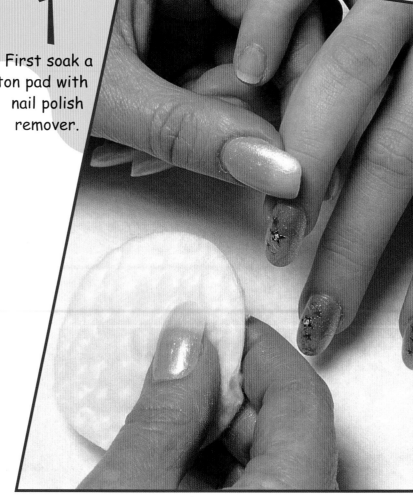

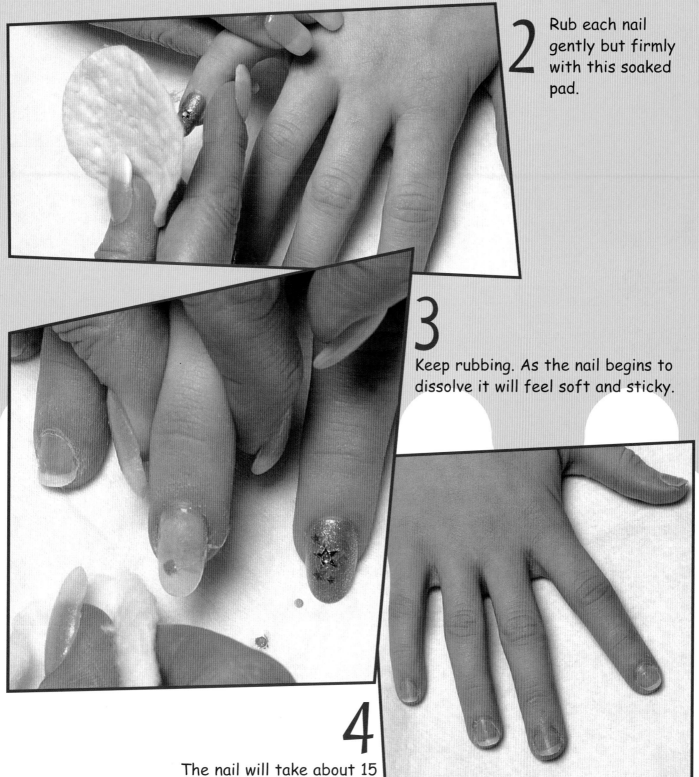

2 Rub each nail gently but firmly with this soaked pad.

3 Keep rubbing. As the nail begins to dissolve it will feel soft and sticky.

4 The nail will take about 15 minutes to remove.

# Index

# Credits and acknowledgements

The Author and Publisher would like to thank the models for their patience and dedication.

## Becky Davis:

A special thank you goes to Becky for her personal input into creating some of her own designs. Even at the age of 12, she has a natural flair and talent and likes nothing better than working in the studio with Marie.

## Rachel Potter:

Rachel has always been a regular visitor to the studio with her Mum, and on special occasions has nail extensions. She is a very lucky girl as her Mum treats her to a professional manicure about once a month.

## Emma Sweetman:

Emma often visits the studio and sometimes has a mini manicure. She loves the mood polishes.

Additional thanks to nail art suppliers Star Gazer for supplying nail art kits that include brush-on nail art sets and additional nail art that has been used throughout this book.